T0158989

CULTURAL FRUITS

CULTURAL FRUITS

Marshella Marshall and Brian Lee

CULTURAL FRUITS

iUniverse books may be ordered through booksellers or by contacting:

iUniverse
1663 Liberty Drive
Bloomington, IN 47403
www.iuniverse.com
1-800-Authors (1-800-288-4677)

ISBN: 978-1-5320-6348-0 (sc)
ISBN: 978-1-5320-6347-3 (e)

Library of Congress Control Number: 2019900271

Print information available on the last page.

iUniverse rev. date: 01/23/2019

BLACK MULBERRY

MORUS NIGRA

BLACK MULBERRY
MORUS NIGRA

BLACK WALLNUT

JUGLANS NIGRA

BLACK WALLNUT
JUGLANS NIGRA

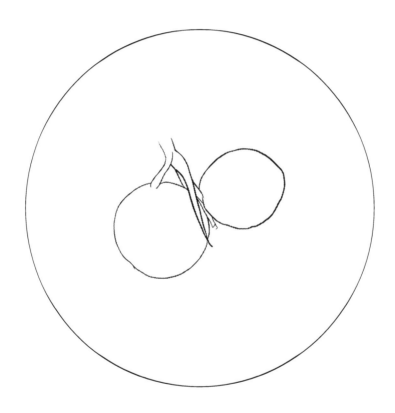

BLACKTHORN

PRUNUS SPINOSA

BLACKTHORN
PRUNUS SPINOSA

BO TREE

FICUS RELIGIOSA

BO TREE
FICUS RELIGIOSA

BREADFRUIT

ARTOCARPUS ALTILIS

BREADFRUIT
ARTOCARPUS ALTILIS

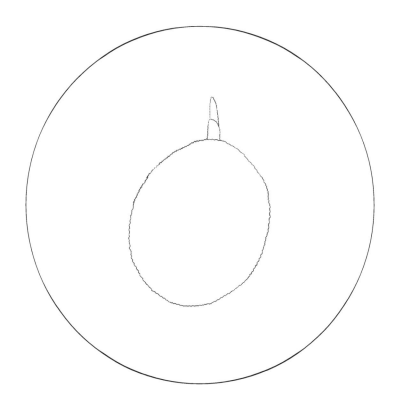

BUTTERNUT
JUGLANS CINEREA

BUTTERNUT
JUGLANS CINEREA

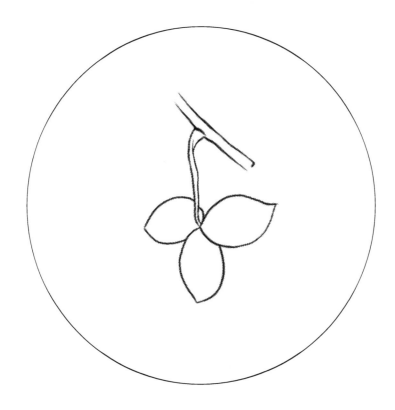

COMMON FIG

FICUS CARICA

COMMON FIG
FICUS CARICA

EUROPEAN BIRD CHERRY

PRUNUS PADUS

EUROPEAN BIRD CHERRY
PRUNUS PADUS

EUROPEAN MOUNTAIN ASH

SORBUS AUCUPARIA

EUROPEAN MOUNTAIN ASH
SORBUS AUCUPARIA

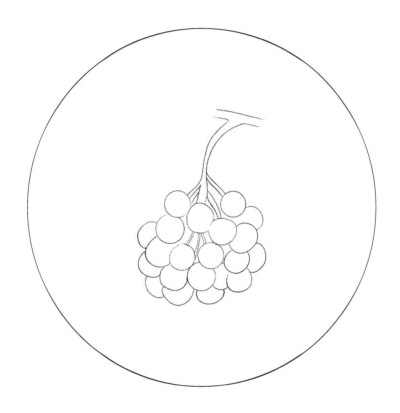

FLOWERING CHERRY

PRUNUS SERRULATA

FLOWERING CHERRY
PRUNUS SERRULATA

INDIAN RUBBER TREE

FICUS ELASTICA

INDIAN RUBBER TREE

FICUS ELASTICA

IROKO

MILICIA EXCELSA

IROKO
MILICIA EXCELSA

JACKFRUIT

ARTOCARPUS HETEROPHYLLUS

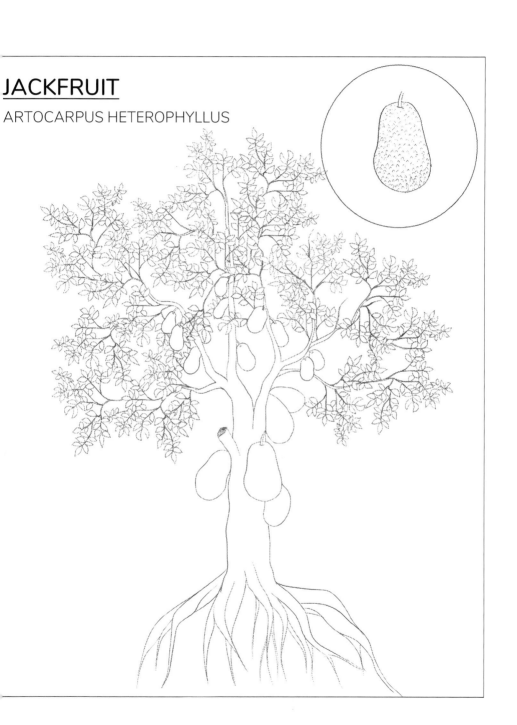

JACKFRUIT
ARTOCARPUS HETEROPHYLLUS

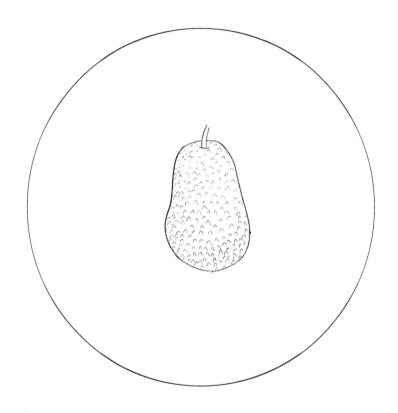

JUJUBE
ZIZIPHUS JUJUBA

JUJUBE
ZIZIPHUS JUJUBA

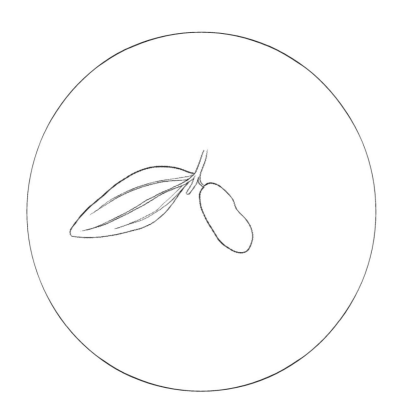

MORETON BAY FIG

FICUS MACROPHYLLA

MORETON BAY FIG
FICUS MACROPHYLLA

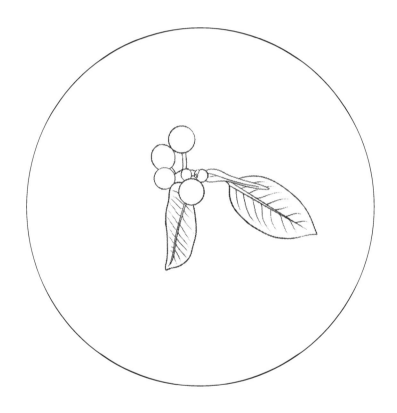

OSAGE ORANGE

MACLURA POMIFERA

OSAGE ORANGE
MACLURA POMIFERA

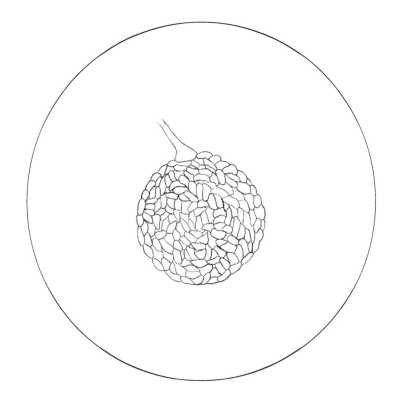

PAPAYA

CARICA PAPAYA

PAPAYA
CARICA PAPAYA

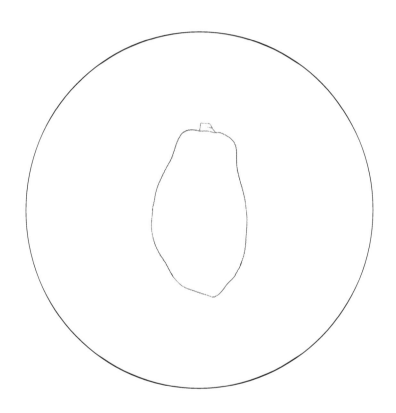

PEACH
PRUNUS PERSICA

PEACH
PRUNUS PERSICA

PEAR

PYRUS COMMUNIS

PEAR
PYRUS COMMUNIS

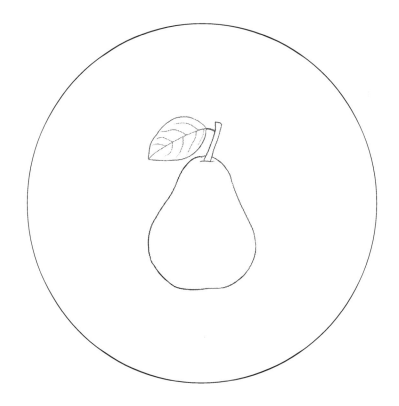

PECAN

CARYA ILLINOINENSIS

PECAN
CARYA ILLINOINENSIS

RAISIN TREE

HOVENIA DULCIS

RAISIN TREE
HOVENIA DULCIS

STRANGLER FIG

FICUS SUMATRANA

STRANGLER FIG
FICUS SUMATRANA

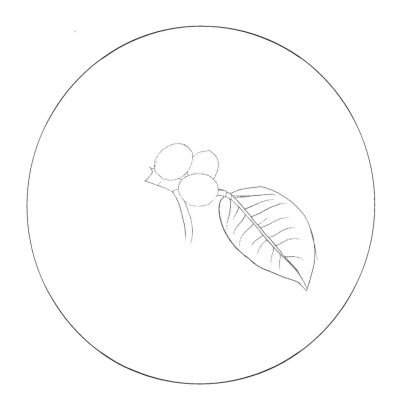

SYCAMORE FIG

FICUS SYCOMORUS

SYCAMORE FIG

FICUS SYCOMORUS

ENGLISH WALNUT

JUGLANS

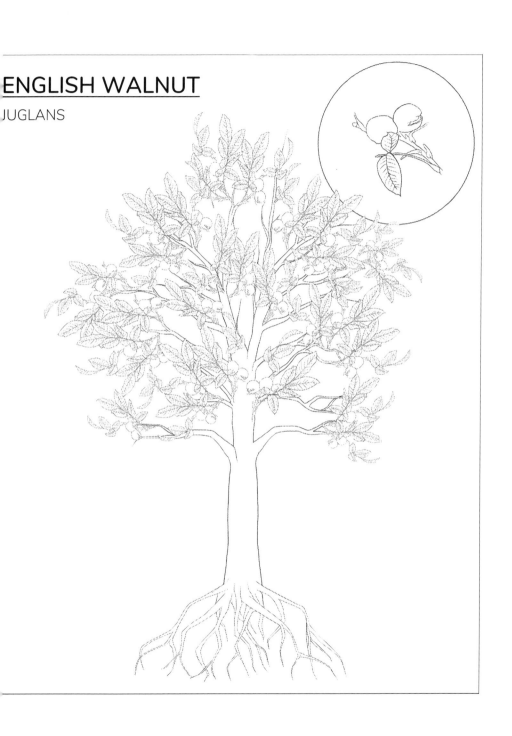

ENGLISH WALNUT

JUGLANS

UPAS TREE

ANTIARIS TOXICARIA

UPAS TREE
ANTIARIS TOXICARIA

WEEPING FIG

FICUS BENJAMINA

WEEPING FIG
FICUS BENJAMINA

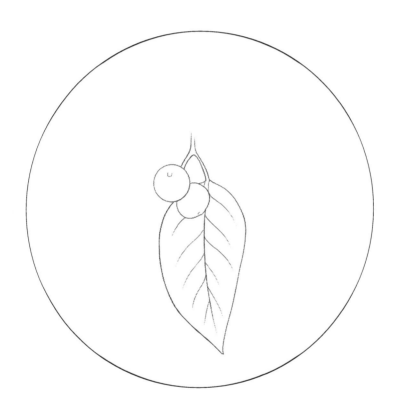

WHITE MULBERRY
MORUS ALBA

WHITE MULBERRY
MORUS ALBA

WHITEBEAM

SORBUS ARIA

WHITEBEAM
SORBUS ARIA

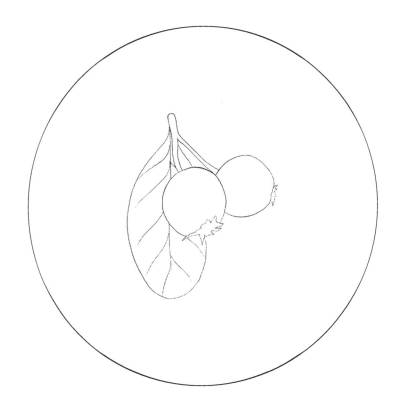

WHITTY PEAR

SORBUS DOMESTICA

WHITTY PEAR
SORBUS DOMESTICA

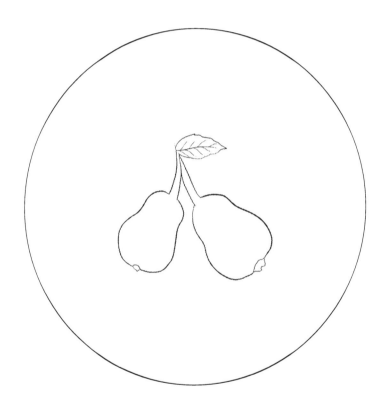

WILD SERVICE TREE

SORBUS TORMINALIS

WILD SERVICE TREE
SORBUS TORMINALIS

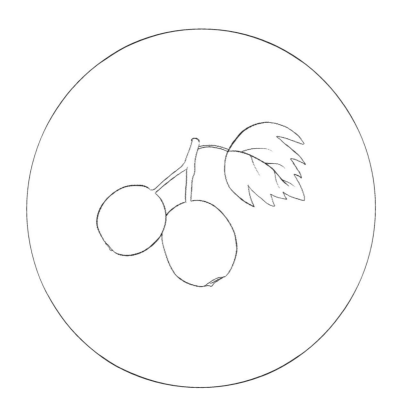

WILLOW PEAR

PYRUS SALICIFOLIA

WILLOW PEAR
PYRUS SALICIFOLIA

WINGNUT
PTEROCARYA FRAXINFOLIA

WINGNUT
PTEROCARYA FRAXINFOLIA

YOSHINO CHERRY

PRUNUS X YEDOENSIS

YOSHINO CHERRY
PRUNUS X YEDOENSIS

Printed in the United States
By Bookmasters